JOMP 17

Edited by CJ Laity

CHICAGO POETRY PRESS

★ ★ ★ ★ ★

Announcing the JOMP 17 Awards

The 2014 Contemporary American Poetry Prizes

$300 Grand Prize: Mary Jo Balistreri, for "Fugue in C# Minor" (pg. 101)
$150 Silver Prize: Anne Wesley, for "no one talks about it" (pg. 85)
$75 Bronze Prize: Jim Davis, for "After the School Shooting, Port Byron" (pg. 90)

The 2014 CAPP Honorable Mentions

Denise Buschmann, for "What Will the Birds Eat?" (pg. 25)
Donal Mahoney, for "So Fingertips Kiss" (pg. 11)
Iris Orpi, for "Six-Lane Catwalk" (pg. 73)
Tracie Padal, for "Grace Notes" (pg. 41)

The 2014 Poet Laureate of Rhyme Award

$100. Jennifer Dotson, Poet Laureate of Rhyme, for "Time Travelers Pantoum" (pg. 58)

Poet Laureate of Rhyme Honorable Mention

S. M. Kozubek, for "The Pump That Could Not Sump" (pg. 59)

The JOMP 17 Poets

Anne Wesley, 85

B. Diehl, 67

Brian Apollo, 65

Bridget McLaughlin, 13, 50

Burjkh M. Halinovych, 61, 62

Catharine Jones, 43

Chris R. Remele, 81

CJ Laity, editor

David Nekimken, 30, 71

Deborah Rosen, 44, 80

Denise Buschmann, 25, 75

Diann Martin, 18

Donal Mahoney, 11, 28

Donna Pecore, 26

Elaine McLaughlin, 35

Eric Lee Messer, 48

Erin J. Green, 93

H. Elle Andrews, 29

Iris Orpi, 73

Itala Langmar, 52, 77

Jennifer Dotson, 58

Jim Davis, 22, 90

JoAnne Blackwelder, 12

Joseph Carey, 15

John J. Gordon, 60

Karen Reynolds, 63

Laura Lee, 95

Laurie Blum-Eisa, 78

Linda Leedy Schneider, 76

Lindsay DiTullio, 34

Margaret Dubay Mikus, 79

Mary Jo Balistreri, 46, 101

Marianne Schaefer, 20

Marian Kaplun Shapiro, 21

Mary Langer Thompson, 45

Mayi D. Ojisua, 16

Michael Schwartz, 57

Nancy Heggem, 32

Pamela Larson, 36

Richard King Perkins II, 49

Robin Goldberg, 19

S. M. Kozubek, 59

Sheila A Donovan, 92

Sheila Elliott, 33

Tamara Tabel, 99

Thelma T. Reyna, 97

Tinamaria Penn, 53

Tracie Padal, 41

Journal of Modern Poetry
Volume 17

Chapter One:
So Fingertips Kiss

Donal Mahoney
Saint Louis, MO

So Fingertips Kiss

Five kids, eight years.
And then one day my wife
shouts to me on the tractor
roaring in the field:

"I've had enough."
And like a ballerina,
she rises on one foot, sole
of the other foot firm

against her knee
and with arms overhead
so fingertips kiss,
she smiles,

pirouettes,
and then like a helicopter
lifts into the air,
whirls over the garage

and keeps rising.
I can do nothing now
but curse
and be proud.

As if at the ballet,
I applaud from the tractor
and blink at the inferno
as she hits the sun.

JoAnne Blackwelder
Ocean City, NJ

Baby and the Moon

For Leeza

You take the baby out to see the moon.
She has heard of the moon but has not
seen it since it has been raining for days.

Tonight is your time, moon rising full,
so bright it burns the clouds away
to wear their silver around its face.

"Moon!" you point. "O Moo!" the baby says,
reaching out, grabbing tight and pulling
your hand so you can cross the street

to get to it. "Moo!" she repeats,
jumping up the sky ladder.
"We can't climb to the moon," you say,

but she will have none of that. A-wail,
she is all feet needing to leave the ground,
and you are heavy, wishing her wings.

Bridget McLaughlin
La Grange Park, IL

Fourteen Ways of Looking in a Mirror

I.
Shimmy past it
in the endless corridor
and steal glances every five seconds.

II.
S t a r e
for hours
into your eyes ...

III.
Admire your beauty
and wonder
who you really are.

IV.
Look
beyond
the surface.

V.
See
what no one else
could ever know.

VI.
Pick apart
and fret about
every flaw that is barely noticeable.

VII.
Pluck
your eyebrows
for hours.

VIII.
Dance
like crazy
in your underwear.

IX.
Mentally
undress yourself.
Then really undress yourself.

X.
Pirouette
Past walls of them
And catch a fleeting glimpse.

XI.
Shatter
the glass
- try not to cut yourself.

XII.
Hog it
for hours
while your family pounds on the bathroom door.

XIII.
Reapply
your rouge
in the women's bathroom.

XIV.
Be daring
and do it
in the men's.

Joseph Carey
Glencoe, IL

The Zip Line

Sitting below the mile-long zip line at Icy Point Straight
sipping on a coke with high grass and tangled plants
a few feet ahead like an impenetrable scraggle of barbed wire
across the Maginot Line as people scream in mid-air
in the distance as if they were on fire and using an old 1920's
college football game cheerleader megaphone to shout for help,
the sounds getting louder and louder until you see their shapes,
sitting in chair-like harnesses attached to the wheels and wires
up above, whipping down the lines like furious freight trains only to hit
the final slow-down hooks at high speed & rock back and forth
like huge crazy bowling pins suspended from strings,
exhilaration glowing on every grinning feature,
so many happy astonished hurled and swinging bodies above our
heads tipped back toward the sky, gazing out along the five
incredibly-long zip line wires curving back up to the mountain and
the sweet heaven skies smiling down around this simple, wind-swirled
event that momentarily mimics the daily speed and sport of birds,
who must surely be watching from nearby trees and wondering
why such loud alien invaders have arrived by cruise-ship to take over
their mighty, wondrous, endless Alaska (and maybe even the entire earth
and moon and sun, for all they know, too).

Mayi D. Ojisua
Chicago, IL

Tangle

what does it take for you
to fulfill another's dream?
is there anything to die for?
where there is loveliness
that's where I want to be.

I came here all by myself.
detained in some kind of way.
before and after the chain.
where fairness takes me,
that's where I would like to go.

we are supposed to be chain free.
wise or foolish beings.
what a foolish one deserves,
the wise will take without conscience.

the other day
I saw a black rose
blooming out of a cracked window.
outside the cracked window,
a red rose tangled the leaves
sprouting from a green seed.

the green seed
tangled a fig tree.
the tree tangled brown tulips,
struggling to bloom.
frayed and tangled flowers
were waiting to be free,
before they die, not knowing
just why they are being chained.

would it not be truly great,
if we were one real family,
with a sense of belonging,
like happy pumpkins
can it not be, when you are holding me,
and I am holding him
we are holding one another,
in one joyful tangle, without any rage or tugging.

instead,
the red tulips tangle with the brown tulips.
The brown tulips tangle with a red rose,
who tangles with the fig tree.

the fig tree is tangled by the hurricane.
hurricane, takes its tangle
to the nearest, tired looking, willow tree.

the soul of a man's heart
is the truth and fruit of his labor.
where fairness takes me
there,
I should go.

Diann Martin
Wilmette, IL

DIORAMAS

Small is good -and intriguing.
Peering into tiny scenes,
Placing self into setting
Oohing and Ahing over the miniatures.
Teenie-Tiny glasses, books, lights and people-
Wine glasses and table cloths,
Candle holders and wall hangings.
Normal but tiny-
Why does the tiny reality make me wonder?
Why do I want to be there instead of here?

Robin Goldberg
River Forest, IL

Tortoise-shell Sight

The woman who makes wildflowers
grows cows in her minivan.

She hums with the radio-
    whistling is offensive.

On runny days
she rockclimbs
and feeds taxes to the caribou.

She laughs at tortoise-shells-
    not comedies.

Her harp rests on her hip
and molds her fingers to the song.

To fill the generation gap,
    she sleeps with nicknames.

Marianne Schaefer
Chicago, IL

Breathless

You've been warned.
Morbid fascination is never a good Segway into romance.
Never mind the thrill of the kill-
Or the shivers and chills you sip from my lips

Death does not become you-
Even in gradual release,
An orgasm at a time,
Your breath recaptured.
Your soul hisses its escape...
Like a tire of the wheel of a toppled bike,
 slackjawed and fearing that the very next ride will be its last

Do I hold the highest honor you can bestow?
Am I the creature whose fingers caress your skin-
Conducting a senate symphony outside and in-
With prickly goosebumps rising to meet their maker-
Applauding my every touch ...?
Each time knowing that loving this much
I will tighten the noose
And, at my whim you will cum, live or die

And this craft that I provide-
As your docent to the heaven between your thighs-
Or the nirvana of the next world yet unseen-
Is not without great sacrifice to me.
You see...
I die a little death with each soul that makes its way down the river Styx,
And the toll of these souls-
Trusting and hungry-
From the eroti-choke cheerleaders guild...
Siren me on.

Marian Kaplun Shapiro
Lexington, MA

What Would I Do Without You?

When
I arc across the double bed
        and there you are *not,*
        it is you in the space
        just as it is you
not at the table
not in the car that is
not in the garage
not next to mine.

If there were no empty space for
your old car you would not be there.
If there were just a single bed, you
would not be there in the space
where you are not. And at your desk
when you are not there, your chair
vacant, your computer sleeping,
you are there in the waiting for you.
Even if you aren't coming home
for dinner. Even if you aren't coming
home at all. In the *n't* of it
there is always the waiting,
my arms *un*met, the words *un*said,
the *not*, the *n't*, the very *un* of you
that I hold on to.

21

Jim Davis
Northfield, IL

Wondrous is the Matter of This Temporary World

The boy lies in bed listening to the negligible sweetness
of rats in the ceiling, tucked in a three flat down the alley
from Hollywood grill, lying still and listening
to the special pleasure of their bodies
so clear to themselves and himself that for a moment
there was no night, no tinny drip of a leaking sink,
only that negligible sweetness, the origin
of which he had to assume. Closer then to sleep, the spirit
of former inhabitants dancing in the spirit of dance,
that which is the thump, the tick, the rhythm of this
fallible meat, this gristled thing hanging over the gutter
of a packing factory, down rows of braided iron
lines above the floor – part concrete, part fire –
where we begin to sizzle and smell like the sound
of a barbaric yawp exploding from the rooftops
of a world obsessed with songs whose saunter through decay
admits that they too are mad about life, remembering that
the flower of harvest which blooms today will die tomorrow
in the ash from which it came. In the years of angels
stacked in ditches and buried, so too there was the rain
which fell on fields of poppy, lily, purple rose, that perfect
impossible field where pollen, wind, bees and great complexities
erupt. Wear your madness like a jacket, make a place for yourself
and live there. There, where the soul stays awake, and the boy
fumbles for his glasses on the bureau, listening to the special pleasure
of small sweetness rustling above – the faith that sleep will allow him
another chance to catalogue whatever sneaks in through the cracks,
down the roof's loose shingles, up the aluminum gutter to find its way
through ceiling fixtures or the dark arcades of the floorboard – faith
that what's mumbled matters the same as the unforgiving rattle
of death, the first cries of life, the vibration in which we believe
that there will be a balance to those killed by drivers, falling ice,
or their own impatient hearts – that the balance will be as simple
as a heart which has made its way through the forest leaving
bits of itself along the path to find its way back – simple as a boy
rolling over, fumbling for a pen, happy to catalogue a sound
in pitch black, straight on through to the subtle hints of morning.

Chapter Two:
What Will the Birds Eat?

Denise Buschmann
Carmel, IN

What Will the Birds Eat?

Wearing a foot of snow
like a high white top hat
on his naked-wood thatched roof,
the little birdhouse,
now aslant,
surrenders
to the glistering
stillness
of our backyard.
The feeder is secured,
dangling in the dip of the iron
shepherd's staff.

This is what the birds see
when they search for seed.

One ambitious cardinal, puffing
herself up like a tiny beach ball,
hunkers down
on the icy
snow covered branch
beside the pole.
She catches me
making out
her yellowish-tan feathers
and dazzling orange beak
through the window.
Eyes lowered,
breath held,
I about-face
with as much stealth
as I can muster
Don't fly away. Please, please stay.
After a moment, I steal a look back.
Only her eyes move.

Donna Pecore
Chicago, IL

What is Missing

aged thin airmail stationary still crisp
unfolds-crinkles-tinfoil-crunch
loud as a dinosaur's roar
in my quiet

found folded within a child's book of verse
dated correspondence
hidden-more than half a century

the sheet so sheer-a frosted glass
started once in ink-leaving
the page blank after the first hello

the space cried for what
unwritten verse
she scribed upon the second sheet
where she dreams of wedded bliss

obvious-a union unfulfilled
the ink her blood
the things that were not
hinted at in this poignant page
wishes of oneness by this lonely one

carefully folding-replacing the fragile paper
 back within the cherished tomb
a onetime baby's gift-complete with dedication
where the name is matched to the letter's end
of this well-read-ragged storybook's nameplate

sharing The Little Red Hen-the first story
(which now, is really the second saga within)
with my grandson Gabe, who discovers "what is missing"
by identifying images placed within the lines

while I imagine images from between the lines
of two who may still live
and wonder who they wed and what they did
and wonder where they are and what kept them apart

and a heavy sadness fills my heart
of what might have been
and think about all the things I have been afraid to start

and think how many miracles were missed
because a letter was hidden
no envelope stamped
a corner not turned
the light shut off
or did they...
because a third sheet was sent?

Donal Mahoney
Saint Louis, MO

Miss Carol's Dumplings

Every month or so
on a Sunday afternoon
I skip the football game
and get in my truck
and drive out from the city
into farm country
to visit Miss Carol
and get my hands
on her plump dumplings.
Biggest I've ever seen.
Best I've ever had,

terrific with her
legs and thighs.
When she lays out
her chicken dinner
on that white tablecloth
I start drooling before
I even get a hand on it.
A farm girl, she says
she's never met
a man like me
so nuts am I

about her dumplings.
Usually, she says,
men like breast meat,
when it's moist,
and I allow how I
like that as well
but not as much
as her plump dumplings
on a Sunday afternoon
and her pluperfect
legs and thighs.

H. Elle Andrews
Chicago, IL

Daniel Island Keep

In a trance, I pace the beach burned to glass,
leaving streams of crimson cream
beneath a cloak of ether steam,
on the shores of Daniel Island.

Standing witness to the trail she stains,
keeping vigil to the tide
that lunges up to bend a sky
it cannot touch, but somewhere meets.

Stranded as widow-bride in barbed wire lace
that cascades in rusted chains
should the maiden ever deign
sip the wine off Daniel Island.

The numbing veil that shrouds my memory
so I can't recall the taste
of the ghost who bore this wake
blows away beyond my reach.

And through hollow eyes, I search the swell,
knowing you can't leave the sound,
swearing in the waves I've found
you in the surf of Daniel Island.

David Nekimken
Chicago, IL

At the Garfield Park Conservatory

I

Green
In all shapes and sizes
Lighter shades commingling with darker shades
Broad leaves spreading shade for the weary
Narrower leaves with outreaching fingertips
exploring their environment
Tangle of arms and legs
tree roots protruding in all directions
Splashes of reds, blues, yellows
erupting from within a long line
of generic green
Caterpillars of color hanging
from leaves' lifelines
upside down
Desert cacti
welcoming simpatico sojourners
warding off perilous predators
Individual expression of life
within generations of genetic patterns
generations of the ancient ways.

II

Art
All life is artistic beauty
Beauty as a panoply of leaf appearances
delicate lace
slender manicured fingernails
broad palms with irregular edges
Beauty as leaves striving
reaching towards the sun
welcoming other species with outstretched arms
searching the earth for essential nutrients.

III

Stillness
A reflection and substance of the Creator
A space for calm inner reflection
A space for merging with all life
The power and beauty of Oneness.

Nancy Heggem
Palatine, IL

Tulip Festival
Washington Park, Albany, New York

Last night's rain washed streets clean as a Dutch housewife's doorstep.

Windows of red brick row houses blink brightly.

Garden club busses queue in the macadam parking lot.

Seniors armed with cameras, pads and pencils walk lanes circling

short wrought iron fences around formal beds.

City crane lifts **"The News"** photographer for aerial shots of

dew shined blossoms standing tall,

each stem caressed by fresh green leaves.

Carmen Rio

Meiscore Angel

Big Purple

Binary Fusion,

Blue Heron Fringe

Super Parrot

Crown Imperial

Sultan of Spring

As I bend for a closer look at ruffled white petals and fringed lavender specimens,

an old gentleman comments,

"Those ain't real tulips like we had in Holland.

See the big red and yellow cups.

My Aunt would gather their hops and cook 'em. Taste like lima beans."

Sheila Elliott

Oak Park, IL

"Scattered Lights, Early Morning"

Early morning and the street is as
shrouded in darkness as a theatre
After a show, thought there are
Intermittent light of varied species
A bulb above a stove that casts a ray
Barely rimming a curtained window's edge. Here is
The suggestive glow of a lamp set close to a wall,
And there, there, a fragment of a beam
Confined to a hallway wall, and
At another home the lamp
Behind drapery casts a sacramental glow.
All this amid the cold and lonely darkness of the morning
For there is only me here, and there, a jogger, and
Perhaps someone hurrying to a train
Down these streets with scattered lights, their intermittent glow
Suggesting someone waits for someone
Else in so many places.

Lindsay DiTullio
Warren, CT

STADIUM LIGHTS

The shivering cold hovers over me
shooting down my arms and legs
My frail, small frame
is outlined by a pale blue light

The light flickers, fades, and blinks
like the fluttering eyes of a camera lens
Opening and closing again to capture fragile moments
Moments that could never be recreated

My silhouette stutters toward the glowing light
Dragging my feet through dark reflective puddles
that drench my slippers in liquid glass

Elaine McLaughlin
Toledo, OH

Dziadzio ze Promesa
(Promise of the Grandfather)

Juden boys, Juden girls

My Polish camera

Monochrome stills.

Emaciated faces, ghost prints on film

My Polish camera, you haunt me still.

Sie kinder eyes, the sunken cheeks,

My Polish camera please don't speak.

Lives burnt forever

Embedded on Nazi film

My Polish camera, you can never heal.

A promise I made on that Victory Day

My Polish camera , Never to touch all of my days.

Sixty years idle, you sat on my shelf, my Polish camera.

Silent reminders of our former selves.

Pamela Larson
Arlington Heights, IL

The Ride Home

My black Honda Accord
bombed with one large deposit of bird poop
dusty dashboard next to an empty Diet Coke can.
Making my way home from numbers and paperclips
shaking my iPod from
The Talking Heads *Same As It Ever Was* to
The B52s *Roam* (where you want to.)
Pulling into McDonald's for a Quarterpounder and fries.

Pity Ronald, once a happy clown
now getting a daily colonoscopy
from a Huffington Post blogger
who is looking to save the world.
Getting up to leave, I hear
Ronald mumble "Damn King can't conquer anything!"
He kicks back a shot of Jack Daniels.
I don't drink

and that upsets Charles Bukowski
How can one like Bukowski and not drink?
To like Bukowski one must know Midleton and Johnnie Walker Blue
but order Cutty Sark
neat.
I rarely bathe with Bukowski.

Nah, ah, ah Steven King get your big toe out of that bathwater!
I can't bathe with someone that takes PAGES to say one shouldn't be wordy.
You'll flatten my Mr. Bubbles and bubbles are important.
Surely, you know that!
I'm going to bathe with Suzanne Collins tonight
she has experience dressing people in flames
to enter a filled stadium.
But I can't sleep with Suzanne

not an athletic Katniss
my ass is too big to balance on a tree branch so
I microwave some Orville Redenbacher's, grab a Diet Coke
and head off to lullabies sung in perfect time and tune by Adrian Monk
remote in hand
I Ken Burns
out of my day

Chapter Three:
Grace Notes

Tracie Renee Amirante Padal

Arlington Heights, IL

Grace Notes

The melody was in my fingers:
I played without thinking,
drawing note after note
from the raw bones
of somatic memory—
Basta! she said.
It was right enough;
and good, but
it was just sound,
just a routine progression
of reflexive movements
that was not quite music.
Music needed sweat, muscle,
soul; music demanded more.
Don't you hear it? The potential,
the subtle shifts: soft here, but growing
louder, gaining strength;
and the notes that whispered
beneath the melody,
the notes that breathed
both within the song
and somehow beyond it,
nimbly slipping between the beats
to split neatly the silence:
the appoggiature, the—
how do you say in English?
She couldn't remember, but she knew
what it meant: *You don't play music,*
she said, *you make it live.*

The essence was already there,
in my fingers. *Once more*, she sighed, *from the top—*
I skimmed the strings lightly—
don't you hear it?—then dug in with the bow:
gaining strength, building the music
with notes that breathed
both within the song
and somehow beyond it—

and when the last trill faded
and my fingers stilled,
she said *yes* and *like that*
and *always!* and at long last
she reached out and turned
the page.

Catharine Jones
Evanston, IL

Dialogue

Dancers mirror our tempted natures,
reflect the *Glengarry Glen Ross* gloss of sharks
in our stunned silence and dive
into our hidden thoughts.
Dancer bodies, undulate, my body imitates
in waves of loose bones and joints,
turn and flex, sweat,
dip, join, slide,
push graceful to jagged edges.

Spines move toe to head and back
swim in black and clouded waters,
then attack. Swift surprise to dredge
small fish people. These bodies become
the sharks' magnanimous culling, and we
fear them or like them become eyes
that stare uncaring, as nostrils
widen, teeth filter and skin glistens.

June 2, 2011: "Sharks Before Drowning" A Molly Shanahan Mad Shak,
Performance at Northwestern University - Marjorie Ward Marshall Dance Center.

Deborah Rosen
Glencoe, IL

21st Century Grammar

I—too burdensome—
don't want to be the pronoun of witness.
WE / OUR dilutes responsibility.
If *WE* kick a 'should' under the sofa
no one is left to pay attention.

WE can minimize, laugh off—
our circle, a round soft cushion.
I is upright thin—
God's finger pointing directly down.

WE all crawl so close to the center
that no one can see while *I,* always capital,
stomps around testifying to the mess
that needs fixing. Crowded so snug,
WE can barely hear God
speaking to the upright we had been.

Mary Langer Thompson
Apple Valley, CA

Alphabet Angst

A cabin in the forest
By a stream, where I
Could philosophize is where I
Dream of being alone
Each day, but like Thoreau a walk away from
Friends and family,
Giving them time with me,
Hellish though it sometimes
Is
Just because it is. I'd have a
Kaleidoscope to look through, old
Love letters to read and
Messages hidden in pine
Needles.
Oh, nirvana!
Please don't bother me, and let me take
Quantum leaps and
Rest, because
Silence is silver and
Try as I might to think otherwise,
Urban is ugly and
Vamping about not for me.
Wisdom in the woods is what I seek, and to exercise my
Xenophobia.
Yes, I'm weird, but I've had *Sex and the City's*
Za Za Zoo!

Mary Jo Balistreri
Waukesha, WI

On the Jetty at Park Shore

In my straw fishing hat, I stand and cast
from the jetty, an arc so graceful it never fails
to give pleasure. Many mornings, in spite
of that lovely arc, and live bait on my hook,
the fish do not nibble.
I dream of snook, of jack,
lifting one from the water on my line,
the pull of muscled arms, exhilaration
of reeling it in, that silvered light on the boulder.
But I never catch many fish. Still
each morning, pole over my shoulder,
bucket and cooler in hand,
I walk down the beach, thoughts ensconced
in a scalloped bubble above my head.
Redfish, bluefish, hurry, bite.

On another fishless day, I rest on a sunbaked rock
and look out over an emerald sea.
Cumulus clouds build towers, shift shape,
climb in the sky's morning glory blue.
Sea salt plays along the rocks,
the air clean and fresh.

I get out my notebook and fish for words.
They swirl around me, above me, but to catch them
is the trick. I cast again and again, sort through
seaweed, pieces of petrified wood, get tangled
in a broken piece of plastic.

A yellow dragonfly, bright as sun, alights on my arm,
wings diaphanous like a ballerina's tutu. I watch
the chocolate eyes, and think
if nothing good ever happens again in my life, I have
lived. And then it flies straight up and is gone.

Suddenly, I'm pulled by a tug
from below. Careful to give the line
some slack, I bring it in easy until
my image stops thrashing.

Eric Lee Messer
Chicago, IL

baboon miming

by tensing the muscles
right below my nostrils
a resemblance
recognizably baboonish
begins to take shape.
my brow pulls down and
upper lip thrusts forward.

i look to myself as if
i could guard something,
and am a little pissed, like
baboons in the parking lots
on television look, chasing
kids for scraps of fast food,
barking guttural insults,
biting the hand that feeds them.

a baboon's politics —
bright red asses,
snapping sharp teeth.

and the poet?

Richard King Perkins II
Crystal Lake IL

Grease Poet

Carl the mechanic
was the first poet
I ever met—
livin' at home
takin' a few classes
at the local CC
I think us younger guys
in the neighborhood
kinda looked up to him
because he was sort
of a regular guy
but when he
came out cryin' one day
and showed us his
first publication
he sniffed that he'd
tried to show
his old man
what he'd done
and all the old drunk
could do was laugh
and drip snot
all over the pages
Carl said this was typical
of how people
treated poets
which was why I knew
I'd never be one
so I asked Carl
to pop the hood
of the Charger
and show me
the spark plugs
or something.

Bridget McLaughlin
La Grange Park, IL

dizzy

dizzy
soars underneath
the scent of slumber

dizzy
kept a piece
of the faded feather

dizzy
foreshadowed
madness

dizzy
had trouble
with the wind

dizzy
churns my living room
into twilight full of mercury

dizzy
thrashes the endocrine
through capillary arteries

dizzy
scavenges the mouse
desperately seeking a stethoscope

dizzy
fumes a throat
to the core

dizzy
mauls the heart
until the sky is in our feet

dizzy
sugars my sister
and heaps herself on me

dizzy
gulps a merry-go-round
release from kingdom come

dizzy
sounds the color
violet in a symphony

dizzy
left fantasy
frothing

dizzy
calls my name

dizzy
never left

dizzy
dreams

Itala Langmar
Kenilworth, IL

To Myself

White uncertain
Vaporous white
White emptiness
Waiting for the
Message to appear
Black restive
Opaque black
Bewildering black
In vain waiting
For no message
To declare.

Tinamaria Penn
Griffith, IN

Venerable Muse

How can I help not to venerate
my old Muse?
Who leads me into foreign places?
I would have not otherwise traveled.

Who is this clever fool?
Who tries me like no other
Transforms my faux pas into smart inventions
Taking me from my reserved thoughts
Making me scream with personification
In a new shape, I listen
As my words are twisted to make them poetically straight
Like the great women writers before me
Makes me wonder if they were visited too
By the same old venerable Muse

Chapter Four:
Hard Working Wordplay

Michael Schwartz
Sugar Grove, IL

HARD WORKING WORDPLAY

I'm a chic sheik with a sleek mystique.
Shrieks of bleak speak critique my technique
with streaks across weeks of tweaks.
These weak creaks barely reach a meek peak
and meet defeat trying to pique disbelief with a sneak peek.

TRAPPED MIND

Too many personalities
to know which one has the authority,
or who has the audacity
to compassionately let me down while relaxing.
One of them grabs me
and begins fastening shackles,
actively harassing me back into fantasies.
It's more than maddening
when I can't understand their vitality.
Grappling with an imaginary sampling
of false personas that leave me stammering.
The fragility of their hammering,
screams understand me,
in a manner that makes me react to it angrily.
Defeat won't come automatically
as their static retreats to the attic sadly.
Perpetual cavities waiting to escape captivity
and wreak havoc passively.

Jennifer Dotson
Highland Park, IL

Time Travelers Pantoum

Time travelers depend on clocks
and calendars to navigate their destination.
Unprotected from the journey's shocks
One must adapt to current conversation.

When compassing your desired destination ·
Last week, two decades or a century ago –
Quickly adopt the current mode without hesitation
Or your strangeness could immediately show.

A week or two becomes decades in the flow
Of time for someone lost in another past.
Don't let your other-time-ness show;
Listen and pick up local jargon fast.

Becoming lost in another past,
It's hard to keep your stories straight.
Listen and pick up the local jargon fast.
Study history and improve your fate.

Some find it hard to keep their stories straight
When suffering time travel's aftershocks.
Remembered history may sway your fate.
Time travelers depend on clocks.

S. M. Kozubek
Chicago, IL

The Pump That Could Not Sump

When I was away,
it rained for days.
Returning to my castle,
surveying the rooms below,
Squish, splosh,
    I water-skied across
the squeaky, soggy carpet.
A pump
    that couldn't sump
    made me a horrible grump
and frightened by the sight
      of the horrible blight, my plight:
water, water everywhere,
    building lumps and bumps and humps,
     but not a drop did my pump sump.
Oh me, oh my, I turn for help,
    "Help!" said me.
"Squeeze me!" said the bloated sponge.
"Dance with me!" cried the braided blond mop.
The plumber quoted a figure,
"I'll drain you sure", said he
    and sure he did:
      in an instant,
      while leaping this hurdle,
      by bubble to burble,
    my savings gurgled,
    squish, ker-plunk, turtle.

John J. Gordon
La Grange, IL

Who Needs 'Em

A self-proclaimed techie snatched a quick look
At the pile of free goodies from which he took
An object he fingered then forcefully shook
Acting as though he'd not seen a real book.

He scanned it at length for the startup icon.
Frustrated he yelled *How does this turn on?*
Try as he may he could not make it play
In less than a minute he flung it away.

The skeptics might say this story can't be
But now kids are wired before they are three
As they become mesmerized by a screen
It lessens the likelihood books will be seen.

Burjkh M. Halinovych

Axis I / Sex / Location

Break the norm, act out, show you're a self-made entity..
Savage bred, parentafied, socialized; reinforced obscenity,
Compared to the status-quot, individually labeled a non-entity,

School and cops crack down; stolen serenity,
Passed through compassion fatigued filtered lenses; stripped identity,
One less problem; census booming and plenty,

Op on the block, look twice; white collar is the enemy..
Three times cycled, hollaring hate is tempting,
Connection, love, worth; empty...

What am I consuming?

No reachable chance on the outside to pleasure me,
Clinical slang jargon, V-code, acuity temp racing feverishly,
Dollar sign on my behavior, no other reason to treasure me,
Diagnostic battery tested assessment used to measure me...

Your staring straight into a barrel of hate,
Misfortune; marginalized fate..
Narrow mind inhibits a hypocrisy you cant escape...

Am I not human?

Burjkh M. Halinovych
Chicago, IL

Confident Serenity

Soundtrack to today's transformative, informative,
no-holds barred non-conformative,
polarizing, thunderstormative..

dispositions and rant-like disclosures...
smug perspective, intensely perceptive...
...disciplined composure..
sitting in a room with no outside exposure..

you cant think.. don't blink..
...or they'll get you..
toss a fancy title on your name tag and follow suit..

walk the line and you'll be fine.. no reason or rhyme..
until you step outside to dine..
...on the attractiveness of liberal thought,
intangible and cant be bought..

...but you want to log experience; your supervision
protects you from the variance..
why are they taking this so serious..?

A broken system enables leaders to value being precarious..

am i delirious..?

If so, call the crisis worker; i must be self-injurious..

Karen Reynolds
Moline, IL

Evolution of me (Love Game of Chess)

Let me clarify-it's not sweet
what started out as angelic turned hellish
a game of chess turned acquiesce
this amateur wrongly calculated on human error
I bet on beauty, charisma and eluding deception
vs. love and long-term integrity
now that they both are gone
it seems the stakes were set on me
through the faltering developments
I should have noticed your threatening schemes
saw that all the faith was irrelevant
when no one had faith in me

I should clarify-my actions were separate from intentions
my movements were pre-meditated
carefully derived from the heart
arrived to a place un-checked
I intended to leave from the start
It would have been less complicated
than cleaning up your useless matter
on board planet "no longer care"
I block out all worthless words
your tactics I no longer share
My visions now clear not blurred

Let me clarify-I had formulated a plan from the beginning
my knight just got in the way
I became a pawn for him to move on
but never intended to stay
arrived at my destination
with plenty of room to bleed
parted with restoration
of love between you and me

I should clarify· It's not sweet what you did
but bitter I am not
for the burn of your harm rang the alarm
brought me back around to reality
I've faced my pain, checked mate with disdain
and found the evolution of me

brian apollo
Maywood, IL

Displaced Honors

Why do we honor people we'll never see
Kicking down the ones that always been there?
In a society that demonizes faithfulness
But delights in hypocrisy and blasphemy
Holy holidays turned commercial
Traditions of love, broken for profit
As foundations crumble and fall
Easier to manipulate those that treasure
And takes pleasure in their own ignorance
Culture erased and replaced by Gucci
So we hang posters of celebrities
The tokens that we've made famous
As long as they don't resist the leash
Placed in a marketed soap box
Made presentable and the ignorant flocked
The wise men left ignored and alone
Or regarded as being irrelevant
Simply because he refused to be
Brainwashed and corrupted by BET
Which sold the "B" and replaced by an "N"
Grandmothers get up on Sunday morning
Sit in service, children playing Angry Birds
The same sit in classrooms
More motivated to spread gossip
Than to take notes for a final exam
The same friends they treasure and call
Becomes the ones that bail when you fall
But I want to be like Lebron or Kobe
Idolizing people who never saw your grades
Never sas you blow out your birthday candles
Would never take you driving practicing
Couldn't care less about your graduation date
But you want to be like the person
Who never knew you even existed

Ignores you on Twitter and Instagram
Yet you commented on everything possible
As the ones that never let you down
Never forsaken you although you have, frequently
They listened to your complaints
Donated the shirt off their own backs
Bankrupted in order to meet your provisions
Would step in front of a bullet for you
Yet you pout and say that's not enough
Because someone else owns more than you
As foundations crumble, as a culture is erased
Skyscrapers of inhumanity replaced tradition
Generations of boys and girls, looking up
To the sold ones in penthouses about to jump
...Culture

Brandon Diehl
Phillipsburg, NJ

My Name is B

Ugly as a blobfish, boring as a desk job —
I can't hold my liquor (or my fingers from their rants).
I've got a balloon for a skull, flytrap-ears,
and charcoal-colored lungs from which I hack up words of phlegm.
I have the attention span of a squirrel and more emotions
than an angsty fourteen-year-old girl with purple hair.

In the nude, I resemble something anorexic;
my metabolism could beat an ostrich in a race.
Damp weather tortures my arthritic mind —
like salt to the slug, acid to your eyeballs.
So mentally, I'm fragile, yes — but even more so morally:
I sneak behind the Devil's back to wine and dine the gods;
I am a swindler — "cheating scum!" some would say.

At the age of twenty-four, I still laugh at farts —
and surely, you can count on me watching cartoons in my deathbed.
I haven't seen a dentist in nine years, and my mother still does my laundry.
And if you want to know the strangest thing about me, here's what you do:

pick a night during one of the coldest months of the year
when my family is out of town. Walk around my bedroom, barefoot
(ideally between the hours of 2:00 A.M. to 6:00 A.M.),
and you'll see it soon enough — you'll know what "it" means soon enough.

So anyway, what do you say?
Will you be my friend?

Chapter Five: We Are Here

David Nekimken
Chicago, IL

We Are Here

Figures crouched in shadows
Appearing frightful on a starry night,
A moral tangle of noblesse neglect
And unkempt contempt,
A lone wolf howling at the moon
For human understanding.

Muffled voices break the silence
Whispering in syncopated beats,
A long history of stifling dissent
And improper etiquette,
Sheep bleating a plaintive cry
For simple acts of kindness.

We are the castoffs, the cardboard citizens,
The cookie cutter people,
Long lives of individual freedom
Turned into corporate crumbs
And tossed onto the scrap heap
Of democratic ideals.

Our voices persist for due process
And immigrant rights,
Screams for our very lives
Reduced to annoying buzzing of mosquitoes,
And chased into bug zappers,
Electric shock for dangerous housewives
And terrorist librarians.

And still we dance!
Our indomitable Divine spirit irrepressible,
An inexhaustible life force
Propelling ourselves past racial bigotry,
Political-religious crusades, and fear.

Stretching our minds beyond rubberband limits,
Opening our arms wide to global fellowship,
Leaping to touch our wildest dreams,
And soaring
As the eagle spreads its wings
And glides in serene self-confidence,
Knowing we are peace and love and joy.

And we dance
Shepherds of our new world order
Stewards of our natural beauty
Stakeholders in our thriving harmonious communities
Spirit connects us all.

We are here, standing tall!

Iris Orpi
Chicago, IL

Six-Lane Catwalk

I stand in the middle
of two-way traffic
in my white dress
a domesticated wild gazelle
unfazed by headlights
moving—
forward,
or back,
depending on
where you're coming from,
what direction you're facing,
hanging note tags on
red lines drawn on
smoky air, post-exposure
through a Nikon with
slow shutter speed
by brake lights
sticking Post-Its of
offhanded judgment on
hexagonal bokeh
filtered blinker beams
through cinematographic
apertures
tunnels that lead away
from extinct dreams
and the facets of a soul
that can't evolve
can't keep up with the times
this is Millennium City
you got to have direction
you got to have power
or the urban tide will
wash over and consume you
pull you down to the
belly of the beast if
you don't know how to swim
Eden is no longer so innocent

this is Paradise lost, then
reconstructed
with stunted palms and
rows of pretty, pretty lamps
the old Eve
a new Adam
and twenty thousand serpents
offering twenty thousand
choices
with which to define yourself
and write your next chapter
so many hearts behind me
zipping accelerated
through the blind night
each with his own reasons
and guiding constellations
so many hearts before me
bloody, beating,
open,
so ready to try
so ready to be hurt
but I've been hurt too and
I respect that,
respect the secrets,
the sheepshank-knotted past,
the scars and the memories
of bruises,
and me your modern, cunning
courtesan, half concealing,
half unfurling all my
monstrous beauty and
the pieces of my broken
piggy bank where I used to
set aside my frugal innocence,
diamond-hungry Satine
from the Moulin Rouge
high-class prostitute
of the mind,
whore of inspiration,
auctioning my golden time
to the highest bidder,
calling out for a muse in
the middle of this
dangerous six-lane catwalk
in my white dress

Denise Buschmann
Carmel, IN

Parking Lot Career Assessment

He's an unhappy soul.
Lumbers like an ape—
head down—
heading for
the teachers' door.

He thinks he could've done better,
I suppose.

I sip my discount senior coffee
in my 12 year old Lincoln,
bundled up in my consignment shop coat,
a few minutes more.

What's he got to be unhappy about?
I gave up the job he has, 30 years ago.

But, I remember those days—
thirty-something
and all the cares of the world—
not realizing
having a good job
should have meant more.

Now, our families raised,
we're the best we've ever been,
we age-group statistics can't get back in.
HR wants us—to support
youngsters like him.

I take my final sip,
prepare to go in
another day and pretend.

Linda Leedy Schneider
Grand Rapids, MI

Halloween in Connecticut

After reading "Twenty Questions" by Jim Moore

Did I forget to look at the sky this morning?
Did I see the flaming dress of the maple soon to be discarded?

Did I honor the honey in my Red Rose tea this morning?
A thick blue mug just like home but no man singing in the other room.

Do I notice the view from my window at the Chester Inn yesterday?
Did I see the reflection of marigold-colored maples in the pond?

Did I see the pond?
Round and perfect as a baby's mouth coming to the breast.

Did I hold my right breast last night, the one that has been crushed
between plates of glass, sectioned, suctioned, cut, the suspicious one?

I know I didn't think of my husband when I woke:
not of spider man, the soldier, or the Dalmatian.
.
Not even of Lily now "too old" to dress.
Lily who carries my name, fears my death.

Itala Langmar
Kenilworth, IL

The White Rose

She had appropriate
Qualifications
He had irreducible specs;
She was refined, *noli-me tangere*
He was courteous, prudent, exacting;
They shared immense
Cultural baggage.
She was agile, intense,
Self-observant, and
Held out her hand
Without trembling.
He fixed his gaze on the void
The splinters and wounds
Of the strange lady's soul
Then gently positioned
A long-stemmed white rose
On the hem of her robe.
The distance between them
Diminished and he began
To forget that
Once long ago
A chess master woman
Had grazed his lips
With her fingers,
Leaving a tiny *sigillo*
To burn.

Laurie Blum-Eisa
Chicago, IL

Lost Daffodils

I imagine that you love another

I see gilded clouds expand
to tempt the vanishing night.
I sing a lilting melody
that curls softly past the dreams.

Teardrops of faded paint
peel from the solid wall,
a lamentation to the never-ending cold
of such a lonely time.

I imagine that you love another.

Margaret Dubay Mikus
Lake Forest, IL

Towards the End

Who knows if
towards the end she
mostly lived vicariously

and that was enough
until the cocooning
to be who she was becoming.

Or if her days seemed full
with the myriad minutiae
vitally important to her

or what used to be
distant memories
that seemed quite real

and that was enough
to get through one day
and another, until…

Deborah Rosen

Glencoe, IL

WASN'T GOD BORED?

Why make humans all alike – two arms, two legs,
forge Adam out of clay and write fini!

Were we in charge, would there not be a tail on some, a hand
upon the head, a pocket in the thigh?

Perhaps God scooped a random round of red clay,
squeezed Adam out then, distracted by all
the whirling worlds, kept creating creatures,
millions per millennia, Adam long forgotten.

If we are powered toward perfection–
eraser on every pencil, "delete" essential,
and God has not returned to tinker,
what would we lose by trying?
Where would we start?

Chris R Remele
Chicago, IL

Transformation of Thought

I thought I was living but I knew I was dead
My essence was draining, leaking making me wish I could see
This wheel I ride was a simple device
Running down the road I knew it would never end
Forgive me for I have but one notion in this world
A crazy time but it spits me in a kind of swirl
The existence of man is my one real legend
The dog came and put its head on my lap
Love so deep I felt it to my bone
Yes now I knew God was here
At last salvation the time for wondering was over
I was really going home
Then the window opened and I was falling
Help, Help I screamed
Only the laughter echoed in my mind

Chapter Six:
no one talks about it

Anne Wesley
Lubbock, TX

no one talks about it

(i. Interruption)

I can't write anything
until I clear a space.
I'm constantly brushing counters of crumbs
and sweeping floors of ragweed pollen
cleverly finding its way inside.
Dust gets its way with baseboards, though:
forgotten about,
out of sight, out of mind.

I can't write anything.
I try to put my hands between my legs
to touch my warmth with my fingertips,
but the space is too clotted
with cellular memories
of intruding, knobby, old knuckles
and a foaming snake
too large to enter.

My space is crowded,
with tender petals peeling off
and flaking pollen dust:
an interrupted bloom and
interrupting my attempts
at becoming me.

(ii. Grandfather)

Poppa's house was balmy
with old people: musty and crumbling.
It was long and low: lots of windows,
and no way out.
Not till twenty years later
did I return, with Poppa safe
in his grave.
But my one slow drive by
the vacant staring structure
nudged around the corners of my brain
and whispered what I'd begun to uncover:
the trees my witness, dumb and accusing.

"Go on now," he'd say
when he was finished with me,
his words thick as maple syrup,
back of throat. Voice slow sap
sliming down the bark of my body.
So I'd go back, sit with my cousins
on the floor for our go fish game:
deal, draw, discard.

"Go on now." And I went,
tucking the lessons into an obscure,
forgotten fold between my hippocampus
and amygdala.

(iii. Gainsaying)

Never again will I love
an albatross.
Handsome is as
handsome spreads his wings
white feathers across my eyelids:
a seal on my memory.

Our honeymoon was short and bloody.
My shoulder skin pierced by his talons,
claw-claiming the nest he twigged
into my scalp while I fast became
that unanchored island
of refuse
roaming the Pacific.

He was a liar, and I swallowed, full stop,
his bird-dropping plots
till his squawks were my maw,
this hideous beak
doomed to repeat
"We're a Harlequin Duck,"
to no one's belief.

I countenanced his betrayal
because I had volunteered
for a quick cawed promise
to forget the slow sap voice.

My albatross.

We plummeted together.
I wore him,
my talisman
for forgetting.

(iv. Reconciling)

I dress with glass and tinsel
the second live fir of my life.
The surprise is how piney it smells;
How thirsty it is;
How proud it bears up under
tarnished, dull ornaments
made from my five-year-old fingers,
heavy already with memoried years;
Its consent to be clothed
in delicate treasures,
popsicle sticks, and electricity,
and still smell of bark and moist earth.

I sit, sleepless, hugging myself
in a six AM darkness
barely warmed by the tiny lights
punctuating the street lamp's glow.
A small hand soft on my shoulder, and turning,
not my daughter's, still sleeping
nearby in her new big girl bed,
but mine.
My three-year old self sits beside me,
small feet swinging, and wide eyes knowing.
She puts her small hand in mine and tugs.
I follow her to the clearing between the window pane
and the Douglas Fir forest
in my living room
where pine needles lift the hair from our necks
and our white toes in snow
wiggle absurdly.
"It's okay to remember now," she tells me,
holding out her hand. "I'm still here."
And I was. And I did, as our small hands
pried from my heart a papier-mâché veil
molded by an albatross promise
for forgetting.

I still have nightmares sometimes—
wet sheet sticky ones that cling to the skin after waking—
of hands on my mouth and a looming moon face
from which there is no hiding.
But I remind myself that I remember
how to clear tangled cobwebs from corners
of my mind, and that we have salve, here
in our own hands.

Jim Davis
Northfield, IL

After the School Shooting, Port Byron

Stockyard where thick stacks of steel
shells sit gritty, crustaceans clinging to a low tide pier,
glittering slightly behind barge traffic – afternoon
rail chug stinks like fuel and salt-decay.

Mid-December and I can't get the heat quite right
so I unbuckle my buckle, pull the sweatshirt over
my head, steering with a knee, temporarily blind,
and I have only just heard of the twenty seven dead.

On an old farm road, a slow green tractor
pulls palettes of reaped soy. The key to long distance
driving is work the cruise and keep your fuel
around a quarter tank. I do. And the Port Byron rest-

stop regulars watch wearily the splintered
screen, turning rabbit ears to fix the picture.
Shame, says the woman wrapped in Karen's apron,
shakes her refuting head, December molasses, smacks

her lips, clicks her tongue, *shit damn shame,* she says.
An oasis of vinyl tables among rows of salted snacks.
I buy Pizza Combos, try on a pair of plastic sunglass
but leave them on the rack. The woman with Karen's name-

tag behind the register tries to smile. Down the road
the red-haired toll attendant's long checkered fingernails
sift bills, sort coins. She's been crying. *Have you heard?*
The world can sure turn you upside down.

I turn on the radio and remember hearing that
on the Mumbai market, blind child-singers fetch more
alms, so eyes, sometimes, are taken.
Fourteen miles to Galesburg, hawks in bare trees

at the junction. I pass a long white van from the Pope
Creek Corrections Department as a girl in the backseat
presses her palm against the window. They're off
to dig ditches on Bliss Road.

They said surviving children, those hidden
behind desks, backs pressed against cold stone below
alphabet chalkboards — cases practiced, capitals
nearly mastered — those hidden survived and were led

from the building hand in hand, eyes closed,
humming the psalms. Follow the song, teacher said —
she has not been told she's beautiful
                              enough. There are holes

in a child's memory. Invention and representation
not yet adhering reality. Capital letters capped
at differing angles, small squiggles of math. Hope,
said Karen, that these are the days they'll soon too forget.

Sheila A Donovan
Chicago, IL

CURIOUS

Cailey, sweet and toothy
Seven years old
With brilliantly weaved braids,
Loves our tutoring sessions.
Deep into CURIOUS GEORGE -
THE BIRTHDAY PARTY,
We giggle at the monkey
Messing up the kitchen with
Broken eggs and spilled cake batter.
George didn't mean to make a mess.
He was trying to help by baking a cake.
I was a child again
Age seven, giggling just like Cailey.

"SORRY FOR THE INTERRUPTION.
WILL MR. PENDERGAST PLEASE COME TO THE OFFICE?
REPEAT, WILL MR. PENDERGAST PLEASE COME TO THE OFFICE?"

Suddenly, the lights in our classroom go out.
Darn! The janitor will have to reset the circuit breaker.
Ms. Conklin, the teacher, herds the
Second graders into the corner, away from the door
Which she has shut tightly, then locked.
Confused, I and the other tutors
Are instructed to join the youngsters,
Already silently huddled in the corner.
It was a practice session
A safety measure.

We await the would-be
Crazed gunman.

Erin J. Green
Chicago, IL

B.B.S.S.
(Broken But Still Standing)
(Black Beautiful Strong Sistah)

Physical abuse delivered by those she believed she loved
and who loved her
Black Eyes
Split Lips

Betrayed by those who promised to never bring her hurt, harm or danger –
friends, family, lovers
Baseball Bats
To the stomach

Sexual abuses she's kept hidden and secret,
praying she can one day forget
Stab Wounds
To the chest

Abandonment by partners; being left to raise the children alone.
To feed, clothe, house, educate and protect any way possible
Gun Shots
To the back

Making ends meet with jobs where the work required far exceeds the pay given
Golf Clubs
To the knees

Yet, she stands before you with flawless skin and a smile
forever burned into your memory
You call her mom, sis or auntie
You might even call her your girl, woman or wife
But, you don't see the scars she wears
Old wounds that have shaped her into the person she is today

She's not bitching......she's venting her pain
She's not fussing......she's fighting to be heard
She's not nagging......she's crying out for help
She is a black beautiful strong sistah
Who's been battered but still standing
She's one of the most resilient creatures known to man
And she deserves your love and respect

Laura Lee
Lombard, IL

Summer in the Swamp

Slope, tilt, then swamp
walk south, towards the dead end
we'd feel our feet begin to sink
smell the pungent green fog.

Forbidden as girls to go
alone into the swamp
we waited until nearly dark--
green mist at dusk
primeval tree downed
we crossed the fetid water:

If you fall in
your skin would melt
your eyes would pop
your hair would turn to green--

But you might meet the witchy woman
beautiful or ugly, young or ancient--
a princess or a witch--
spirit or human, evil or lonely--
somehow not not quite dead.

Colleen said she saw the woman
riding her broom one night
her hair was black and shiny
her face lovely but wild.

Cathy said she's sure she saw
her ride into the swamp,
stop to hunt with a bow, then leave.
Helen said she's sure she saw her
flying low, into the ground--
then a coyote scared her off.

We crossed the swamp, arms linked
four girls at a time
afraid to look down
hearts pounded sweat trickled--
always summer in the swamp.

Jeff and Micky, Tom and Rusty
laughed, said there was no woman at all--
But we girls knew better--
even boys did not enter the swamp alone.

One evening we four girls hid
watched the braver boys,
cross over the swamp on the dead tree,
holding onto each other's sweaty shirts--
startled to see
they looked down as they crossed,
they dared to look down--
but would not say what they saw.

Thelma T. Reyna
Pasadena, CA

CROSSING

"People see scavengers... another human being has fallen.
We accept it as a way of life. You know it's going to keep on going on."
--Los Angeles Times, "Corridor of Death," 6-23-13

1

a faded shirt impaled on brambles,
shoes tilted by the rutted road, laces caught with thorns and webs,
the water jug crumpled and coated with sand.

the texas rancher wipes his brow,
squints into heat shimmying from dirt and rocks.
no vultures, no wild hogs screeching and tearing at flesh.
this death is old.

he picks his way through scrub brush and mesquite,
dust swirls eddying up his boots. he knows the body's here,
somewhere, somewhere close by —
more bones and desiccated flesh to count,
more human detritus to unearth and wonder over.

amazing how quickly dreams suck into themselves and die,
how bodies young a day before cannot survive the push,
the trek, how legs collapse among these brutal stones and melt,
how brothers let their kin give in, to stay behind and perish
under cactus and this satan sun.

"corridor of death" they call this god-forsaken swath
between the border and the end of dreams. corridor of death,
where nations meld, one and the same, vastness on one side
blurring to the other, miles and miles that beckon and destroy.

under tangled branches of oak, the rancher sees a hand, bloated fingers
curled to the sky, a wedding band glinting in shadow.
the young man is shirtless, his eyelashes matted with dust,
bare feet and thighs gnawed to the bone by badgers and raccoons.

how quickly life snuffs out when promises betray, when hopes collide
with land that must be crossed, that must be broken through, earth and
dust and sand and stones and thorns and sun and all the innocence
that kills, when all this must be crossed, and maybe dreams survive
on this other side. but this death is old. each death is old.
the rancher lost count so many years ago.

Tamara Tabel
Barrington, IL

Remembering My Father

I. Surgery

He awoke
glanced
at the clock
whispered
Not enough time.

Not time enough
for surgeons to
carve
out
the cancer

just long enough to
open
look
shake their heads
thread the needle.

I have no regrets
he said
as we sat
on that sterile
hospital bed.

But now
years later, I
wonder
want
for all left
unsaid.

II. What Remains

I stand before his dresser
in summer, stare
at his life in
a single drawer:

a self-winding watch
simple wedding band
money clip, a cheap
gold-painted pill box

army pins and badges
from the Korean War
a fragile set of saké cups—
his souvenir of Japan.

I long for something
to hold, snatch the cold
metal container, turn it
trace its sharp edges

mourn for his touch
his laughter, his warmth
the room silent and still—
an empty box.

III. Reconstructing Dad

I piece together bits of him
like notes scribbled in black felt tip
on torn corners of restaurant napkins.

But the memories and stories make
an odd, misshapen man—
an elephant man with cascades of skin
a primordial dwarf with a mouse's snout
an amputated rendering

    not him at all.

Mary Jo Balistreri
Waukesha, WI

Fugue in C# Minor

I watch my father's covers rise and fall as fists
of wind knock oleander against the patio door.
      The sky darkens
and rain pelts the house like shrapnel.
      Blue light flickers from the TV, photos
            of dead soldiers flash on the "News Hour"
                one shot at a time.

His bony body, swaddled in fleece,
        sits in a beige arm chair,
            legs lifted to a pillowed coffee table.
In his hand, an orange Popsicle
        as bombs flare across the screen.
            Sirens wail in the distance.

Dad's small voice asks for ice chips.
            How baffled he must be with the turn
                his life has taken, how the view keeps changing,
                    one slide after another.

Walking into the kitchen, I think today—especially difficult—was
        a wall of black, like looking at a written fugue for the first time:
            extricating separate voices from the polyphony,
                trying to discover what each distinctive voice says,
                    its impact on the others,

a C# minor day, all tension and intensity
        when I had hoped for a reprieve, just a small change,
            an orange blossom scent, a buttercup glaze
                on those White Mountains in the distance.

I turn off the news, listen to Bach on the stereo. We sit
in silence. The monsoon quiets
        and my father closes his eyes.

CHICAGO POETRY PRESS

Made in the USA
Charleston, SC
15 June 2014